THE DATING

JUNGLE...

WHICH ANIMAL ARE YOU ?

LOL PUBLISHING, LLC
2009

The Dating Jungle
LOL Publishing, LLC
2009

Copyright © 2009 by Russ Stevenson

Illustration copyright © 2009
Michael Auger - Arty4ever.com

First Printing 2009
ISBN: 978-0-9825212-0-5

Printed in the United States of America

DEDICATION:

E. Joseph Cossman,

Mentor and Friend

Gloria Stevenson,

Mom made this all possible

Kathleen Birmingham,

Understands how to turn chaos into

a best seller

Acknowledgments:

Any book takes a great deal of time and effort to put together, and most authors find they really cannot do it entirely alone.

I wish to thank my colleague who read portions of this work for clarity, and Michael Auger for his fantastic cover art.

PREFACE:

Welcome to **THE DATING JUNGLE**, This is a fun-filled, lighthearted book designed to help you understand yourself in regard to your personality and traits when looking for a loving partner.

As you probably know, there are many variations of teachings regarding the personality traits that are common grounds to attracting someone you want to date, live with, or marry. This book is intended to be fun, and to give you a new way of viewing yourself or a potential partner. It is not a manual to self-enlightenment.

Let's get started!

~Russ Stevenson

CONTENTS:

Introduction

Even back in the dimmest mists of recorded history, human beings have always spent a great deal of time in the pursuit of finding an ideal mate. We've all seen the old cartoons that would have us believe that it was once not only possible, but socially acceptable to bop a woman over the head and drag her home. Apparently, the act of bopping was the Stone Age equivalent of exchanging rings—and there are women in the world who still feel that many men never got the memo that such behavior has become passé.

THE ARRANGED MARRIAGE

As the eons passed and human beings began to become more "civilized," one of the hottest trends in "dating" became the arranged marriage. It may have saved women from the headache of being clobbered by a caveman, but it did little to encourage the interaction between the sexes—unless you count the interaction between the parents who were busy arranging the marriage.

Two sets of parents got together and negotiated the terms of marrying a son and daughter to each other, even if the two children had never met. It didn't seem to matter—to the parents, at least—that their kids might possibly end up fighting like proverbial cats and dogs and be unhappy for the rest of their days, since divorce was pretty much unheard of at that time. What was important was that either peace was maintained between the families or sometimes between entire kingdoms—or that one or both of the children would benefit in some substantial way from the arranged marriage.

That system lasted for centuries—and still goes on to one degree or another even today in some parts of the world—but eventually most of the world finally decided that maybe it was better to just "let nature take its course" when it came to courtship. If a male and female liked each other, they'd find a way to connect. Most young people thought that was a terrific arrangement, but it meant they'd have to take much more responsibility if their choice of a partner turned out to be the worst decision anyone ever made.

HARDER TO MEET YOUR MATE

As we enter the twenty-first century, a growing number of single people are facing problems that are unique in human history. Our social organization is breaking down, the long-established ways that boys and girls (or men and women) used to meet each other have virtually disappeared, and human beings are finding themselves feeling more isolated than ever before. As the Internet entices people to stay home and connect in cyberspace, face-to-face contacts are becoming fewer and farther in between.

In big cities, nearly everyone is from somewhere else, which means the shared sense of values and background has also been lost as more and more people move to urban areas. That has complicated the dating process even further, since each area of the country and each ethnic group has its own history and ways of looking at the world.

INTERNET DATING

So how do you try to narrow down your choices when it comes to potential mates? You could join one or more of the hundreds of dating sites on the Internet and hope for the best, but then you'll always run the risk of running into the situation described in the famous cartoon that shows a dog sitting at a computer keyboard, typing happily away in a chat room.

As a second dog looks at him questioningly, the first dog says with a smile, "On the Internet, no one knows you're a dog."

There's an uncomfortable amount of truth in that simple statement. If you're articulate enough, you can come across as anyone—or anything—you like on the Internet. Then, as long as no one sees your picture, you can be anybody you say you are—until that moment of truth when you finally meet face-to-face with whoever you've been talking to.

Depressing, you say? Scary, you say? It could be, but there have been many attempts over the years to sort out life's "possibles" from life's "no ways." A couple of the most interesting ideas involved separating personality types into groups, based on birth dates and birth years.

CHINESE ZODIAC

One of the earliest, and it's been practiced for nearly 5,000 years, was the Chinese zodiac. For all those millennia, the Chinese zodiac has tried to predict how a person's personality will turn out, based on their year of birth. Of course, if that theory is correct, a person has to wonder about the consequences for teachers who are faced every year with an entire classroom filled with nothing but Roosters, Rats, or Pigs. Given that all of the students in each grade were born in the same year, shouldn't every child in each new class possess exactly the same characteristics? The chances are, that's not the case, even though the Chinese zodiac system is still believed and practiced after nearly fifty centuries.

ASTROLOGY

A second attempt at categorizing personalities is nearly as old, dating back to Babylonian times, but it took a much different approach. Instead of lumping people into entire years, it broke the year down into twelve months within that year. Over the centuries, that system has remained popular, partly because a sizable number of people do seem to find at least some similarity between how a person feels and acts and their birth sign. Of course, you can take it with as many grains of salt as you wish and it's probably not a wise idea to plan your daily life around what you read in the horoscope column of your local newspaper.

There have been many other systems over the centuries, as well, including a Native American system that used totems and animal spirit guides that have attempted to simplify the incredible variety and complexity of human personalities and the interactions between people by identifying and labeling them into groups.

DISCOVER YOUR PERSONALITY TYPE

In this book, you'll be able to explore your own personality type, based not on the year, month, or hour of your birth, but on your actual personality traits and preferences.

The key to using the information in this book most effectively can be found by taking it with as few or as many grains of salt as you want. There's no real scientific basis or background for the animals you'll soon read about and the human personality traits associated with them. The most important thing is: *have fun with it all!*

As the title of the book suggests, in some ways human beings still haven't managed to move beyond their distant jungle-dwelling ancestors when it comes to the search for an ideal mate. When it comes to the quest for finding compatible people, the phrase, "It's a jungle out there," is every bit as true in the twenty-first century as it was for Og back in the Stone Age. Of course, you generally no longer have to carry a club around if you're a male looking for a mate, and you'd probably be safe to assume that you're not in any imminent danger of having to suffer even a glancing blow from a love-crazed club wielder if you're a female.

Getting Started

The information you're about to explore in the following pages contains descriptions of twelve jungle animals, both pro and con, with no judgment attached. Each animal will be described in detail—but only AFTER you've answered some challenging questions about each of twelve "mystery" animals. In other words, you'll be answering the questions BEFORE you find out which animal was being described.

TEST FIRST, EVALUATE LATER

After you've totaled up your "Yes" answers for each of the twelve mystery animals, you'll be able to move on to see which animal most closely describes your particular personality. Don't be surprised if you find that you have two—or possibly three—animals that best fit your personality. After all, human beings are multi-faceted creatures and we all have qualities that can vary according to the situation.

For instance, you may feel like a lion in one situation and a lamb in another, yet those qualities are both part of your makeup. In other words, no one is always one particular animal at all times—you may have strong characteristics of one species, but there may be times when you'll also exhibit other behaviors that may be more in character with an entirely different animal.

Other interesting (and fun—remember, this is supposed to be fun) suggestions you'll find in the descriptions will be the animal personalities that you'll find most—and least—compatible with the animal you most closely identify with. This can help you make more informed choices when it comes to choosing your next love interest.

BOTH PARTNERS SHOULD TAKE THE TEST

If you're currently in a relationship, you can have your significant other take the tests, too, and see how they view themselves. Another fun activity would be to take the tests, using what you know about the other person to discover which animal you think most closely resembles their personality. The results can be very surprising—and can encourage some deep (and sometimes hilarious) discussions.

The bottom line: *enjoy this!* Just like the Chinese horoscope or the Western version that is so popular today, the jungle animals in this book are meant to offer just another way to seek compatibility in other human beings—and especially in people of the opposite sex. Don't accept or reject anyone based solely on this information. You may wish to maintain a degree of skepticism about its truth and validity.

Now that you know the concept, let's get started in your quest to find out which animal best describes you—and remember:

"It's a jungle out there!"

Taking the Animal Tests

Now it's time to see which animal you are in this jungle we call a world. There are twelve animal tests, each representing a specific personality type, and there are twenty questions to each test. Don't give them a lot of thought. In fact, it's best if you don't think about them more than a second or two—your first reaction is probably the correct one, so go with that in most cases.

On a separate sheet of paper, or by making photocopies of the "Animal Tests Tally Sheet," that you can find in the Appendix of this book, place a hash mark every time you answer the question with a "Yes."

After you've finished a test, tally your "Yes" answers and then move on to the next animal test. When you've finished all twelve tests, look at your highest scores to determine the number of the animal that best matches your personality type. Then look in the descriptions to see which animal corresponds to that number. You'll probably be surprised at how well that animal describes you!

Results

Don't be surprised if you end up with the same number of yes answers on two different tests. All that really means is that you have strong characteristics of both animals. First and foremost we're human beings, which means we're complicated individuals and not easily categorized.

Following the animal descriptions, you'll find a Compatibility Chart for all twelve animals, giving you further insights into which animals are most compatible with you—and just as important, which animals to avoid! Compare your results with those of your partner. Are you compatible?

Animal Number One

1. Are you a patient person—until someone pushes you too far, at which time you can be somewhat unpredictable in how you're going to react?

2. Do you pride yourself on your ability to observe things in their smallest detail?

3. Are you rather quiet and reserved in social situations?

4. Are you somewhat uncomfortable in the spotlight?

5. Do you consider yourself a considerate, loyal friend?

6. In a crisis, do you usually remain calm while others are losing their heads, trying to figure out how to resolve the crisis in the most logical, rational way?

7. Do you set high standards for your own behavior, only to be disappointed when those around you don't live up to your expectations?

8. Do people sometimes think you're aloof and dispassionate, when what they're

really seeing is your emotional balance mixed with calmness and common sense?

9. Do you generally work hard at solving a problem and then stick to it until you've accomplished your goal?

10. Do you do better as a leader rather than a follower in most circumstances since you believe in your own ability enough to think you can best assess the situation?

11. Are you a good problem solver?

12. Do you tend to view situations in black-and-white, good or bad, right or wrong?

13. When someone is rude or insensitive to you, do you usually withdraw and try to figure out what's going on rather than confronting them?

14. Do you pride yourself on showing your affection for someone by doing many small kindnesses?

15. Do you feel deep passion when you're in love but have trouble showing it on the outside?

16. Do you prefer to perform acts of kindness for your lover instead of making flowery romantic displays?

17. When you're in love, are you faithful and expect your lover to be the same?

18. Do you bury yourself in your work or some other activity when you've suffered a broken heart?

19. Are you liable to take your time when it comes to falling in love rather than rushing into relationships?

20. Do you pride yourself on not being the jealous type, as long as your lover treats you with the same loyalty and respect you give them?

Animal Number Two

1. Would you describe yourself as honest, loyal, and sincere?

2. Do you have a strong sense of duty—to your job, your family, and your friends?

3. Are you usually the first person to speak up when you see an injustice being perpetrated?

4. Are you usually willing to sacrifice your own ambitions and desires to help those you love live better, more fulfilling lives?

5. Do people look up to you because of your altruism and interest in bringing justice and fairness to the world?

6. Do people tell you their most intimate secrets, knowing you'll never tell anyone else?

7. When you feel threatened, do you sometimes lash out, becoming judgmental and defensive?

8. Do you sometimes get criticized for complaining about things over which you have no control?

9. When you're in love, is one of your greatest joys knowing that you're needed?

10. Do you pride yourself on your honesty—especially when it comes to love relationships?

11. When you're in a loving relationship, do you find yourself worrying that you're not doing enough for your lover?

12. Have you ever lost a lover because they felt overwhelmed by all you tried to do for them?

13. Do you have a calm demeanor that sometimes belies how you're really feeling inside?

14. Do you have a great sense of humor that seems to make people comfortable with you right away?

15. Since you genuinely think you know best in most situations, do people sometimes think you're somewhat bossy?

16. Do you have a healthy respect for tradition—to the point that you sometimes have trouble dealing with change?

---

17. Will you generally stand beside your friends and loved ones during difficult situations, ready to fight, if necessary?

18. Can you just "smell" a phony through some sort of sixth sense that you find hard to explain to others?

19. Do you rely on intuition more than logic when it comes to sizing up other people's characters quickly?

20. Do most people who really know you seem to like you unconditionally?

Animal Number Three

1. Do you have a strong sense of what you want out of life?

2. Do you just seem to attract a group of people who are willing to follow you without having to put out much effort on your part?

3. Are you persuasive enough that you rarely lose when it comes to a debate?

4. When your persuasiveness isn't enough to convince the other person, do you sometimes use intimidation to win the day?

5. Do you sometimes hold grudges against people who have angered or hurt you in some way?

6. Are you comfortable in the limelight, being the center of attention?

7. Do you find yourself fairly attractive to the opposite sex, to the point where you don't have to work very hard to find potential relationships?

8. Even though members of the opposite sex find you attractive, are you quite selective

about who you strike up a love relationship with?

9. Do you prefer to live alone rather than in a relationship that is less than what you want for your life?

10. Are you good at motivating other people to complete projects you have initiated?

11. Do you see yourself as a leader?

12. Are you good at recognizing opportunities and taking advantage of them?

13. Do people sometimes mistake your self-confidence and enthusiasm for being egotistical?

14. Do you often find yourself challenging authority?

15. Do you tend to wear your emotions and feelings on your sleeve?

16. Do you find yourself moving too fast at times and have to remind yourself to slow down and smell the roses every now and then?

17. Do you set high standards for yourself and then expect others to live up to them, as well?

18. Do you sometimes blurt out secrets before you can stop yourself?

19. When things aren't quite going as you planned, do you sometimes find it hard to ask for help?

20. Are you happiest when you have a worthwhile goal to work toward?

Animal Number Four

1. Do you consider yourself creative and artistic?

2. Are you somewhat insecure when it comes to love relationships, needing to be reminded how important you are?

3. Do you shy away from confrontations if there's any way to avoid them?

4. Do people ever compliment you on your good manners?

5. Do you ever find yourself daydreaming, which affects your ability to stay on task?

6. When crises arise, are you more likely to let someone else take charge?

7. If someone makes a decision you don't agree with, do you quietly go your own way without confronting them about it?

8. Are peace, order, and security among the things you cherish most?

9. Do you sometimes have trouble concentrating on the minute details of a project, preferring to leave those small details to someone else?

---

10. Do you try to surround yourself with nice things—without breaking your budget?

11. Do you feel inexplicably depressed if you aren't surrounded by beauty, whether it's man-made or a work of nature?

12. Do you love to study the various religions and philosophies of the world—especially the New Age and metaphysical?

13. When it comes to actually practicing a religion or philosophy, do you prefer not to have to put too much effort into it?

14. When you're in a love relationship, do you sometimes have difficulty making your needs and desires known?

15. When you set out to find a new relationship, is being financially stable one of your higher priorities?

16. When it comes to courtship, do you appreciate receiving romantic gifts and sentimental little notes?

17. Do you normally prefer a candlelight dinner to a walk in the woods when you think about your personal definition of a romantic date?

---

18. Is one of your highest priorities finding someone who will often tell you how much you're loved and appreciated?

19. Are you fairly generous when you're feeling good about yourself but tend to withdraw, both emotionally and physically, when you're feeling somewhat insecure about yourself or your relationship?

20. In your overall relationships, do you consider yourself a good team player?

Animal Number Five

1. Do you just seem to attract people of both sexes to you by the strength of your winning personality?

2. Do you sometimes find yourself being thrust into the spotlight, even though you haven't necessarily sought the limelight yourself?

3. Do people tend to see you as being somewhat philosophical and seem to listen to what you say without your having to press the issue?

4. Do you sometimes have difficulty with people falling in love with you even though you haven't given them any real encouragement?

5. In the past, have you sometimes found yourself a bit oversexed simply because of the availability of willing partners?

6. Would you say that your sense of humor is among your most attractive traits?

7. Do you find yourself using a combination of your heart and your mind when it comes to choosing a new lover, rather than just listening to your heart and rushing in?

---

8. When you find yourself interested in a member of the opposite sex, are you hurt—but surprised—when your advances aren't appreciated?

9. Even if your initial advances aren't returned, do you continue to pursue someone when you've decided they're the one for you?

10. When you're involved in a relationship, do you find other people still pursuing you, even if you haven't sought other company?

11. When a love relationship has ended, do you sometimes still find yourself jealous of your ex-lover, even though you may not still love them?

12. When making a business or investment decision, do you size up the situation in terms of a combination of intuition, instinct, and thought, rather than on strictly cold, hard facts?

13. Are you basically cautious with your finances?

14. Do you prefer activities and jobs that allow you to use your mind rather than requiring a great deal of physical effort?

15. Do you enjoy a lively discussion in which there is friendly give-and-take?

16. Do you find yourself occasionally having to stretch the truth or even not telling the truth if it means getting yourself out of a difficult situation?

17. When someone does you a significant wrong, do you sometimes carry a grudge?

18. Do you have an almost uncanny knack for staying calm in the midst of a crisis until the crisis has been resolved?

19. Do you like to surround yourself with the finer things in life, including original artwork?

20. Do you tend to collect things that interest you?

Animal Number Six

1. Do other people seem to look up to you for leadership?

2. Do you generally gain respect in your dealings with others, even from people who may be on the opposite side of an issue?

3. Are you more prone to stand up and fight for the things you believe in, rather than settle for less than what you think is fair?

4. Do people sometimes think you come across as somewhat aloof and distant?

5. Do you generally have the ability to put up a calm exterior appearance, even when you're feeling a fair amount of turmoil inside?

6. Are you really a softie at heart, even though you can put up a fierce façade in times of crisis or danger?

7. Do you sometimes think you're too brave for your own good, which can get you into trouble?

8. Do you live by the philosophy: "If you want someone to do it right—and on time—you've got to do it yourself?"

9. Does money just seem to come to you as a byproduct of doing the things you love to do?

10. Do you seem to have an above average ability to attract attention from members of the opposite sex?

11. When you're in a loving relationship, do you expect your partner to stand by your side as you work hard to make your own way in the world?

12. Do you have a fairly strong libido that you sometimes have to keep in check when flirting with members of the opposite sex?

13. Are you drawn to lovers who are a bit more docile and allow you to make most of the decisions?

14. Do you sometimes do unpredictable things when you're faced with an unexpected new challenge?

15. Do you occasionally find yourself rubbing authority figures the wrong way, even if you didn't mean to do it?

16. Do you find it difficult to simply stand idly by when you see an injustice being committed?

17. In your career, do you most enjoy those times when you're able to do a job your own way without interference from supervisors or advice from other employees?

18. Are you known for your sense of humor, even though people sometimes have to take a moment to realize you're joking with them?

19. Do you sometimes think that a solitary life would be preferable to having to constantly compromise in a relationship?

20. When you're not feeling well, do you like to be pampered by someone?

Animal Number Seven

1. Do people just seem to like you because of your gentle, kind personality?

2. Do you consider yourself unusually lucky?

3. Do you find the creative arts to be one of your favorite pastimes?

4. Would you describe yourself as basically a conservative type of person?

5. Do you like to dress nicely, that is, a cut above the average person?

6. Do you enjoy decorating your home with artwork, especially works that you've created yourself?

7. Do you find that people tend to forget about disagreements they've had with you relatively quickly?

8. Is it difficult for people to argue with you simply because you refuse to allow an argument to get started in the first place?

9. When it comes to love relationships, do you find yourself being pickier than many of your friends and associates?

---

10. When you're looking for a potential partner, do you look for someone with a combination of good looks and sensuality, coupled with financial stability?

11. Do you consider yourself to be a sensual person?

12. Do you often wear your heart on your sleeve, making you prone to crying at times?

13. Are you known as a laid-back sort of person in your workplace?

14. Do you sometimes have a tendency to be excited about a project initially, only to abandon it before it's been completed?

15. Do you have a tendency to find creative ways around obstacles rather than confronting them head-on?

16. Do you pride yourself on being a good negotiator, finding win-win situations rather than concentrating on winner-take-all?

17. Do you sometimes adopt a slightly naïve and vulnerable exterior to give you an advantage in certain situations?

18. Are you generally turned off by people who seem to live their lives surrounded by an excessive amount of drama?

19. Could your life motto be summed up by saying something like, "To each, his own?"

20. Do you derive a strong sense of inner peace from the fact that you have a healthy self-image and are confident in your own abilities?

Animal Number Eight

1. Are you generally a person who sums up the old adage, "What you see is what you get?"

2. Do you pride yourself on always giving your best, regardless of the circumstances in which you find yourself?

3. Do you like to open doors for people and generally show politeness and civility in most situations?

4. Do you sometimes find yourself getting fooled by people who seem bent to take advantage of your giving nature?

5. Do you have a strong belief in the basic goodness of human beings?

6. Do you derive your greatest pleasure in life from doing things for other people?

7. Have you ever sacrificed your own comfort in order to do something for the sake of someone else?

8. Do you sometimes have difficulty graciously accepting kind gestures or gifts from other people?

---

9. Are you often reserved when it comes to speaking your mind until you're certain that the other person is genuinely interested in what you have to say?

10. Do people sometimes mistake your reserve, good manners, and civility for being snobbish or stuck up?

11. Do you have a particular love for fine dining?

12. When it comes to love relationships, do you sometimes find yourself being a bit too overprotective and jealous?

13. Do you have a somewhat "naughty" side that you only show to your lover?

14. Has your generosity and willingness to please ever clouded your judgment about a lover's true personality and intentions?

15. Are you sometimes too hard on yourself when you make a mistake—a true perfectionist at heart?

16. Are you uncomfortable in the limelight, preferring to work behind the scenes to get projects completed while allowing other people to bask in the glory?

17. Are you relatively tolerant with the faults of others, but not quite as tolerant with those you find within yourself?

18. In negotiations, do you typically just lay your cards on the table and deal from a position of honesty and openness?

19. Are you an avid reader and watcher of nonfiction television that will enrich your mind by obtaining new knowledge?

20. Are most of your friends people you've known for a long, long time?

Animal Number Nine

1. Would you describe yourself as energetic and active?

2. Do you love doing things that involve crowds, such as sporting events, concerts, or live theatre?

3. Do you sometimes find yourself finishing people's sentences for them because you already know what they're going to say?

4. Do you sometimes pretend to be a little slow if it will give you a competitive advantage during a negotiation?

5. As a young adult, were you eager to get out of your parents' house so you could start life on your own?

6. Do you sometimes find it hard to be a "team player," since you're usually eager to get a project done and hate having other people slow you down?

7. Does your ego get in the way of your good judgment at times?

8. Do you occasionally find yourself suddenly losing interest in a project and wanting to move on to something else?

9. When it comes to attracting members of the opposite sex, do you make it a special point to use your physical attributes (whether you're male or female) to their fullest advantage?

10. Do you sometimes feel as if you have less control over your life when you're in a love relationship?

11. Do you find yourself acting uncharacteristically illogical when you're involved in a love relationship, doing things you wouldn't normally do?

12. Have you ever ended a love relationship because someone was applying enough pressure to make you feel as if you were losing your freedom to be your true self?

13. Do you have a rather well-developed stubborn streak that sometimes gets you into trouble?

14. Are you sometimes bothered by wanting your independence yet also wanting to belong at the same time?

15. Do you have a seemingly tireless energy when it comes to accomplishing a goal that means a lot to you?

16. Do you often find yourself growing restless for no easily explainable reason?

17. In your choice of a career, did you seek something that allowed you to work directly with people?

18. Are you comfortable being center stage?

19. Does your mood sometimes change quickly, causing you to lash out at others before you've had a chance to clearly think it through?

20. Do your friends and associates think of you as someone they can give a project to, knowing that you'll throw yourself into it wholeheartedly?

Animal Number Ten

1. Do you consider yourself one-of-a-kind when it comes to your dress and overall style?

2. Have people occasionally characterized you as being a dreamer, even though you have a strong practical side, too?

3. Do you love to wear relatively flashy clothes?

4. Do you love shopping for bargains when it comes to your wardrobe?

5. Do you pride yourself on being completely transparent and honest in your dealings with people?

6. Does your honesty and candor sometimes get you into trouble?

7. Are you hard to deceive because you seem to have a sixth sense that allows you to spot phonies?

8. Do you have a hard time just sitting and watching a television program without doing something else at the same time?

9. Are you relatively prudent with your overall finances?

10. Have you ever had a love relationship end because the other person just seemed to fall short of what you'd always believed your "dream lover" would be like?

11. Do you find particular happiness in knowing that you're attractive to the opposite sex?

12. When it comes to finding a new love relationship, do you tend to fall in love at first sight?

13. When you're in a relationship, do you often like to have your lover remind you of how attractive they think you are?

14. Do you sometimes find yourself tempted to stray from a love relationship simply because members of the opposite sex find you attractive?

15. Do you enjoy being in the limelight?

16. When you're at a party, do you often find yourself the center of attention — the life of the party?

17. When you're involved in a negotiation, do you state your case right up front and then fight hard to persuade the other person to adopt your position?

18. If the negotiation is going quite badly, do you finally retreat, sometimes accompanied by great frustration?

19. Do you sometimes see a paradox between your outside appearance and the way you feel deep down inside?

20. When you give someone your word, will you do everything in your power to make sure that you keep your promise?

Animal Number Eleven

1. Do you think of yourself as a person of definite contrasts?

2. Do you have people in your life who you consider more as acquaintances than real friends?

3. When you have a problem to deal with, do you generally prefer to work it out yourself without much input from other people?

4. Are you a particularly busy person who likes to be on the go most of the time?

5. Is traveling one of your favorite pastimes?

6. When it comes to your life, do you generally like to live by your own set of rules and standards?

7. Do you enjoy being both mentally and physically active?

8. Do you have trouble holding on to your money, causing you to feel financially strapped at times?

9. When you're on vacation, do you often find yourself buying small souvenirs that aren't particularly useful to help commemorate the trip?

---

10. Have you been burned in the past by investing money in a risky business venture or get-rich-quick scheme?

11. Do you love shopping hard and finding bargains on the things you want?

12. Do you conceal a fairly sensual inner nature by assuming a cool public façade on the outside?

13. In unstructured situations, are you likely to stay relatively quiet and in the background?

14. Are you known by your close friends and family members as having a good sense of humor?

15. Do you love to read?

16. Do you sometimes have to control your temper when it suddenly flares for no easily discernable reason?

17. Do people often tell you their secrets, yet they don't really know any of yours?

18. Do you consider yourself a good problem solver?

19. Are you able to keep your head during crisis situations until you can diffuse the problem?

20. Do you tend to get edgy and nervous when you're upset at someone or something?

Animal Number Twelve

1. Are you generally cheerful and friendly?

2. At a party, will you usually be one of the people who keep things lively and fun?

3. Do you pride yourself on your ability to be able to see the good side of almost any situation?

4. Would people who know you describe you as vivacious and gregarious?

5. Do most people seem to like you from the first moment they meet you?

6. Do you sometimes hide your real emotions under a friendly, cheerful outer façade?

7. Do you consider yourself a good listener?

8. Do your friends often turn to you for advice on their problems?

9. Are you naturally curious about nearly everything around you?

10. Are you generally unaffected by what other people think about you?

11. Have you ever had a love relationship end simply because you got bored and wanted to explore other opportunities?

12. Do you love to stay active, both mentally and physically?

13. Do you have certain foods that you simply can't seem to get enough of?

14. Do you find yourself maintaining friendships with a variety of people because you don't have any one friend who shares all your interests?

15. Do people sometimes think you're nosey, when all you really are is intensely curious?

16. Do you get a lot of the things you want simply because people seem to want to do nice things for you?

17. Do you have a special knack for picking up tasks quickly and being able to perform them well without a great deal of effort?

18. Do you consider yourself unusually lucky?

19. Do people sometimes have difficulty knowing how you're really feeling deep inside?

20. Are you generally comfortable in the spotlight?

What's Next?

Congratulations! You've completed all twelve animal tests.

Now it's time to tally your "Yes" responses, and find out which animal you are, and which animal(s) you're most compatible with.

On the next page is a quick-reference table that shows the correlation between each "Mystery" animal and the Jungle Animal who most easily represents you.

After you've found which Jungle Animal you are, read further to learn more about your personality and traits for that particular animal.

Then, proceed to the next section, which shows the animals you're most compatible with, and those that you should avoid or look at cautiously when considering a love relationship.

Again, this is all done in fun...so enjoy it!

Let's move forward.

Animal Number One	Water Buffalo
Animal Number Two	Elephant
Animal Number Three	Gorilla
Animal Number Four	Giraffe
Animal Number Five	Hippo
Animal Number Six	Lion
Animal Number Seven	Tree Frog
Animal Number Eight	Warthog
Animal Number Nine	Zebra
Animal Number Ten	Parrot
Animal Number Eleven	Gecko
Animal Number Twelve	Chimpanzee

Water Buffalo

Animal Number One

INTELLIGENT, POWERFUL, HIGH-ACHIEVERS

Water Buffaloes are solid, dependable, and powerful creatures, high achievers, and good leaders. Because they're hardworking, responsible, and patient, you may get the impression that Water Buffaloes are slow and dull, but that's not the case. Once you get to know them, you'll find Water Buffaloes to be highly intelligent, keenly observant, and detail-oriented. They're capable of original and creative thinking, which also makes them good problem solvers.

QUIETLY PERSEVERANT

In social situations, Water Buffaloes are quiet and reserved. They're not party animals and generally don't seek the spotlight. They wouldn't be comfortable there, anyway. A Water Buffalo is the kind of person you want by your side in an emergency, as they are loyal, confident, and protective of those they love. In a crisis, they remain calm and sensible, formulate a creative solution, outline the logical steps to face it, and then work tirelessly to bring about a solution. Water Buffaloes never give up until their goal is accomplished.

BLACK AND WHITE THINKERS

Some people may have trouble understanding Water Buffaloes because Water Buffaloes tend to see things as black or white, good or bad, right or wrong. They set high standards for their own behavior and believe in living a moral, virtuous life. They also expect others to behave properly, which means they're often disappointed. Holding others to their own high standards can make Water Buffaloes seem to be judgmental and inflexible.

ALOOF BUT LOYAL

Water Buffaloes are usually emotionally well-balanced, although people who don't know them may think they're aloof and dispassionate at first. They can be difficult to get close to, but once they include you in their group, they're loyal, and supportive companions who always deliver on their promises and never let their friends down. Water Buffaloes are generally patient and slow to anger, but if you push Water Buffaloes too far, they may react impulsively and their fury can be fearsome.

KIND, CARING, SURPRISINGLY SENSITIVE

Under normal circumstances, Water Buffaloes are kind and caring. They're close to their families and will do almost anything for their friends. They can sometimes be overly self-sacrificing, and can end up disappointed when others don't seem to appreciate or reciprocate their kindness. They're courteous and considerate in their dealings with others, and if they're treated with rudeness and insensitivity, Water Buffaloes will be surprised, hurt, and angry. They generally withdraw from people who have been unfair or inconsiderate to them, and if the affront is serious enough, they can sometimes be provoked into making an aggressive attack.

EFFECTIVE LEADERS

Since Water Buffaloes are hard and steady workers, they generally excel in their chosen career, and they often become respected and effective leaders. They expect others to work as hard as they do, and to behave responsibly, which means they can sometimes appear to be too demanding or judgmental. Because they are highly intelligent and are blessed with lots of common sense, they usually think they know best and don't appreciate being told what to do. Fortunately for them, they're usually correct in their assessments of situations, which is another reason they do better as leaders than followers.

LOYAL LIFE PARTNERS

Water Buffaloes can make wonderful life partners. They're loyal, committed, and protective of their chosen mates. While their emotions are deep and passionate, they may not show it on the surface. They can be tender and sensual lovers, but they're not adept at flowery romantic displays because they just don't see the need. They demonstrate their devotion every day through selflessness, hard work, and unwavering fidelity.

Water Buffaloes are the least likely people to be fickle or unfaithful. Once you've won their affections, Water Buffaloes will stick by you—as long as you're willing to do the same. Although they're not normally the jealous type, Water Buffaloes feel they have a right to expect loyalty and consideration from their mates, because that's what they'll offer in return.

CAREFUL WITH THEIR HEARTS

If Water Buffaloes get rejected or betrayed, they take their broken heart and withdraw, tucking the hurt away inside and devoting themselves to their work. It may be some time before they open up again. Fortunately, this isn't likely to happen over and over with Water Buffaloes because they're generally very good judges of character and don't jump into new relationships quickly or without thought.

Although that attitude may create an impression of coolness and a lack of spontaneity, it's their way of shielding their hearts and protecting the deep passions that are hiding just below their calm surface.

BE WATCHFUL FOR THEIR SMALL ACTS OF LOVE

Trouble can arise if Water Buffaloes don't find partners who understand that their many small sacrifices and hard work are their way of expressing their love and devotion. Lovers of Water Buffaloes may sometimes miss the love behind those small acts and try to gain more attention by nagging or sulking, but Water Buffaloes won't understand such behavior. Instead, they'll be hurt and bewildered, and they may shut down and withdraw while they try to figure out the situation. While that's going on, their partner may begin to look elsewhere for the romance and excitement they feel they're missing, setting up a chain reaction that can destroy even a long-term relationship. Water Buffaloes can become vulnerable to crushing disappointments in their middle years if they allow their relationships to unravel in this way.

IDEALISTIC, FAITHFUL, VERY STUBBORN

Water Buffaloes are hardworking, methodical, steadfast, and intelligent in their dealings with others. They're confident in themselves and their abilities and never compromise their ideals. They're faithful, reliable, and affectionate with friends and lovers, and they treat strangers with courtesy and fairness. They're strong leaders who inspire others to excel. They can sometimes be stubborn and unyielding, however, and may have difficulty understanding those whose behavior fails to meet their own high standards. If they can overcome their inherent rigidity, especially when it comes to their personal relationships, Water Buffaloes are destined to be able to live a long, happy, and successful life.

Water Buffaloes are most compatible with Parrots, Geckos, and Hippos. However, if Water Buffaloes are paired with Chimpanzees, conflicts are likely, and relationships with Giraffes or Warthogs will result in constant misunderstandings. Lions are the worst match for Water Buffaloes, since they're both powerful leaders—and when they clash, neither will back down. However, in the end, the Lion will usually be driven away in order to survive.

Elephant

Animal Number Two

LOYAL, QUICK TO DEFEND

Elephant people are honest, sincere, and possess a strong sense of loyalty and duty. They sincerely enjoy helping others and are usually among the first people to speak up whenever they feel that an injustice is being done—especially to someone they love. You can always count on Elephants to be there when you need them. In fact, Elephants are always ready to jump to the defense of those they love, whether it's a verbal or physical attack. Elephants are humanitarians and strongly believe in equality.

WILLING TO SACRIFICE

Elephants are true givers, willing to sacrifice their own desires and ambitions for the sake of those they love. Their innate sense of decency and fair play makes them champions of the underdog, and they'll do whatever they can to help even out an unequal situation.

ALTRUISTIC, GOOD SECRET KEEPER

Elephants inspire confidence because of their altruistic ways, and that confidence is well earned because they'll work tirelessly to try to bring balance to the world around them. Their loyalty and genuine interest in other people brings them many close relationships, built upon empathy and sincere warmth. Since their friends know they'll do anything for them, Elephants are generally held in great esteem by all who know them. Elephants are also good listeners and can be trusted with your most intimate secrets. Elephants don't go in for gossip or idle chitchat.

EXCELLENT COMPANIONS...USUALLY

Paradoxically, Elephants make great companions—unless they're in a bad mood. When feeling threatened, Elephants can lash out and become judgmental and defensive. However, if you treat Elephants with the respect and fairness they deserve, they continue to be the best friends you could ever want or need.

MELLOW WITH AGE

Elephants aren't necessarily social creatures, but they make wonderful one-on-one companions. When they're young, Elephants can be a bit over the top as far as complaining about things over which they have no control, but that's just because they haven't learned which things they can influence in their lives and which ones they can't. As Elephants grow older, they gain a better sense of perspective and tend to mellow considerably.

TRUTHFUL AND FAITHFUL

When it comes to romantic relationships, Elephants tend to seek out people who will make them feel needed. They're generous and honest to a fault, and they're most comfortable when they feel needed. So in romantic situations, they're usually the giver and the object of their affection is the taker. However, an Elephant's lover will always know they're being told the truth at all times. Elephants are fiercely monogamous—they don't play games when it comes to love.

ANXIOUS ABOUT LOVE

Unfortunately, all of those honorable qualities can sometimes lead Elephants to have a hard time when it comes to finding and keeping a lover. Since Elephants are worriers at heart, they're always concerned that they may not be doing enough to show their affection. That anxiety can cause them to go overboard and cause their lover to feel overwhelmed and smothered at times. Even when Elephants appear to be calm on the outside, they're often nervous and apprehensive on the inside—Elephants never seem to be able to fully relax.

PLAYFUL, HUMOROUS, STUBBORN

However, Elephants can also be playful and disarming, and they have a great sense of humor, which makes people—including members of the opposite sex—like them almost immediately. Attracting lovers isn't an Elephant's problem—it's holding on to lovers that's the hard part.

Since Elephants genuinely believe they know best, and they can sometimes come across as being bossy. They may also appear to be aloof, mainly because they're introverts and rarely show their true feelings unless it's absolutely necessary. They can be stubborn, too, because they know what they want and are eager to get it in the most efficient, and quickest way possible.

CYNICAL, PESSIMISTIC

Elephants can become cynical because of their altruism and they can sometimes say sarcastic things, brought about by their basically pessimistic attitude toward life. Since Elephants are the ultimate givers, they rarely expect to receive a whole lot from the world in return.

TEACHER AND GIVER

As they grow older, Elephants often become pillars of society, holding offices and pursuing careers that make them trusted and revered by everyone who knows them. They make excellent spiritual leaders and teachers, because they genuinely want to give everything they've got to create a better world, in spite of their sometimes dim view of society's ills. Since they're so honest and likeable, Elephants are often boosted in their careers by important people along the way. On the other hand, Elephants are one of the least materialistic of the animals and don't seem to worry about accumulating money or attaining great success. However, since people like them so much, Elephants are generally prosperous. Their tastes are usually simple and fairly easy to fulfill, even on a modest income.

NOSTALGIC AND FAITHFUL

Elephants respect tradition and sometimes find it hard to adapt to change. Since change is hard for them, they can sometimes become overly nostalgic about the good old days. Elephants can mistrust people they don't know at first, but once you have gained an Elephant's friendship, you'll have a friend for life.

PROTECTIVE, INTOLERANT OF INJUSTICE

Elephants are protective of their friends and loved ones, and you can always count of Elephants to be honest and straightforward. If you have an Elephant as a friend or lover, you never have to worry about having to face a difficult situation alone. Your Elephant will be there at your side, fighting tooth and nail to make sure no harm comes to you. Elephants have a strong tendency toward seeing the world in black-and-white, and they'll sacrifice life and limb to correct whatever injustices they perceive. Once they've decided upon the rightness of an issue, they won't rest until that wrong has been righted.

PERCEPTIVE, INTUITIVE

You can't fool an Elephant with social graces or pretensions. They're intelligent, perceptive, can smell a phony, and can see through dishonesty with a nearly unerring sense of intuition. One of their strongest traits is their ability to judge a person's true character.

SEEK TRANQUILITY

Elephants can do well in business relationships with Lions because of their mutual love of truth and justice.

However, when it comes to true compatibility with the opposite sex, Elephants will have their best luck if they look to find Tree Frogs as life partners.

A Tree Frog will give an Elephant the serene, tranquil life that an Elephant needs in order to be happy. Since Elephants are worriers at heart, they need a calming influence to help them balance their need for balance with their pessimistic attitude about ever being able to achieve that balance in their lives.

Elephants will have the least luck with Gorillas, who are often too proud to put up with an Elephant's criticism.

Elephants will also have difficulty trying to be in love (or even business) relationships with Giraffes because they don't have time to put up with a Giraffe's whims and occasional selfishness.

Gorilla

Animal Number Three

POWERFUL, INTELLIGENT, PERSISTENT

Filled with vitality and a love of life, Gorillas are some of the most powerful people, especially in the strength of their personalities. Gorillas are generous, intelligent, and persistent. They know what they want out of life and work hard to reach their goals.

LIKES BEING THE CENTER OF ATTENTION

They often collect a band of devotees as they make their way through life because they're comfortable being the center of attention in social situations and can be very persuasive. In fact, it's very difficult to win an argument with a Gorilla. If their logic isn't persuasive enough, Gorillas can sometimes become intimidating through the sheer strength of their personality. It's not a wise idea to arouse the anger of Gorillas because their vitality and persistence will cause them to keep after you for a long time, especially when they genuinely believe in their side of the argument. Whether their actions are positive or negative, Gorillas attract attention and are constantly in the limelight. A Gorilla's many admirers are usually eager to hear what their lusty friend has to say, and when it comes to handing out advice, Gorillas aren't shy.

LUCKY IN LOVE, NEVER LONELY

Gorillas are generally lucky in love, since their lust for life and flamboyant style naturally capture the attention of the opposite sex. Although Gorillas are emotional people, that doesn't mean they're necessarily sentimental or overly romantic. It's really a Gorilla's style and personality that other people find irresistible. They simply take it for granted that people will like them. When it comes to love, Gorillas are generally the heartbreakers and not the other way around. If they can't find someone they feel meets their standards, they'll wait for the right person, and if they don't find them, Gorillas are often content to live alone. After all, their magnetic personalities attract lots of people, so they're seldom lonely.

STRONG, CONFIDENT LEADERS

Gorillas are great for initiating projects and for motivating people to stick with a project until it's complete. As leaders, they often appear larger-than-life and have the ability to inspire confidence in their followers. In fact, Gorillas are confident enough in themselves to believe that it's their destiny to lead the way.

KNOW HOW TO USE POWER
AND INFLUENCE

All that means is that Gorillas will often accumulate considerable wealth and material goods, although the pursuit of wealth isn't really what drives them. They simply are good at recognizing opportunities and have the enthusiasm and self-confidence to take advantage of those opportunities when they arise. Gorillas are constantly searching for ways to increase their power and influence—not necessarily just for material gain, but because it's in their nature to do so. Gorillas see themselves as leaders and take that role very seriously. They constantly challenge authority until they finally reach the top, and once they've attained the heights, Gorillas know how to stay there. Crossing a Gorilla is rarely a good idea.

STRONG EGO, INFLEXIBLE, STUBBORN

On the negative side, Gorillas can come across as egotistical, although if you ask them about it, Gorillas will often say people mistake their self-confidence and drive as ego. However, Gorillas can be inflexible, due in part to their ability to recognize opportunities and quickly devise plans for taking full advantage. That quickness can get in the way of what others would call common sense at times when Gorillas allow their enthusiasm to overrule their judgment. Gorillas can sometimes be stubborn and irrational, and it's generally not difficult to know how a Gorilla is feeling—their emotions are evident and they don't even try to hide them.

LIKE TO SAY, "I TOLD YOU SO."

Although being a quick-thinking go-getter can inspire admiration in others, Gorillas sometimes lose their perspective during their quest for success. At such times, they would do better to try to slow down and smell the roses. Learning to appreciate life's little things can go a long way toward gaining a greater sense of balance in a Gorilla's life. Gorillas can also benefit from showing more compassion and tolerance to those people who admire them. Although they can be supportive, they're also among the first people who will say, "I told you so" when things start to unravel—especially if a project is falling apart because of taking a different approach than the Gorilla originally suggested.

ECCENTRIC, DEMANDING, GREAT LEADERS

Because of their zest for life, Gorillas are often seen by others as eccentric and demanding, but they may not see it that way. Because they demand a great deal from themselves and hold themselves to a higher standard than most people, they have a tendency to expect others to share those high standards. It's hard to live up to such demands, so Gorillas sometimes find themselves surrounded by admirers who aren't necessarily close friends. Being the boss can sometimes be a lonely existence. Gorillas can make excellent politicians, doctors, ministers, or public speakers, since they're comfortable in leadership roles and being in the spotlight. If anything, they may sometimes stick their foot in their mouths because they're outspoken about their beliefs.

LOYAL, UNABLE TO KEEP A SECRET

Gorillas are loyal to their family and friends, and when someone needs help, they can count on a Gorilla to be there to do whatever needs to be done. They'll tell you exactly what they're thinking, and since their minds are constantly in motion, they will sometimes blurt out secrets, so you may want to be a bit careful about what you tell them if you don't want it generally known.

CAN BE TOO QUICK TO TAKE ACTION, GOAL ORIENTED

Since Gorillas are action-oriented, they expect other people to hold up their own end of a bargain. That need for action can sometimes get Gorillas into trouble if they don't analyze a situation carefully enough. In their rush to take advantage of a situation, they may overlook flaws in their plans—and live to regret their hasty decisions later. Since they are confident in their abilities, Gorillas will sometimes overextend themselves, but that same self-confidence can prevent them from asking for help, which can lead to exhaustion and potential health problems. Gorillas are always searching for a worthwhile goal or cause to work toward. Without something to reach for, a Gorilla just doesn't feel fulfilled.

When it comes to compatibility, Gorillas get along best with Geckos, but they can find happiness with Hippos, as well. The two least compatible signs for Gorillas are Warthogs and Water Buffaloes, who both have a hard time understanding the sometimes excessive vitality Gorillas display.

Giraffe

Animal Number Four

CHARMING, ELEGANT, ARTISTIC

Giraffe people are charming and attractive, elegant, creative, and artistic. However, they're often somewhat insecure and feel the need to be loved and protected. When they're drawn into complex predicaments, generally against their will, they try hard to shy away from confrontation and pull back when faced with having to take an unpopular stand.

FUN TO BE AROUND, OFTEN LATE

Since they're well-mannered and peace-loving, Giraffes are generally fun to be around, making them popular people, as well. They're free thinkers, lovers of nature, and often tend to be dreamy and disorganized—and they're sometimes even a bit lazy. They're frequently late for appointments, which can make other people become impatient with them at times, but their gentle and compassionate nature is so endearing that they soon put everyone at ease again.

ANXIOUS, INDECISIVE

Since they can be overly anxious and pessimistic at times, which can make them hesitant and indecisive, you'll rarely see a Giraffe as a great leader or a captain of industry. They're more likely to be followers, respecting authority and rules, and eager to avoid conflict as much as possible. They'll let other people make the big decisions, although they generally won't support a decision they don't agree with. They love peace, order, and security, and usually won't do anything that will create disharmony or discord.

METHODICAL, CREATIVE

Methodical, linear-thinking people may have trouble understanding the whimsical Giraffe.

They're often inattentive to minute details and disorganized in their work habits. In addition, Giraffes will often gravitate toward creative or artistic careers, in which they can excel. They can also make good salespeople or consultants, because those careers allow them to capitalize on their natural wit, charm, and pleasant personalities.

ENJOY GOOD LIFE AND LOOKING GOOD

Although they love fine things, Giraffes aren't really all that interested in accumulating a great deal of material wealth. They have a strong appreciation for the good life, but they don't necessarily want to mortgage their souls to achieve it. Giraffes appreciate beauty, both in themselves and in their environment. They want to be surrounded by comfort and beauty as much as possible, so they'll often spend an inordinate amount of time in front of the mirror, making sure they always look their best. They also have a strong desire to live amid lovely surroundings, so much so that they can actually become irritable and depressed if that's not possible for whatever reason.

RELIGION HAS ITS PLACE

Giraffes are often drawn to the study of religion, partly because of their difficulty with making their own decisions, and they can be drawn to New Age philosophy, horoscopes, and the occult. Whatever beliefs inspire them, Giraffes limit their involvement to practices and religious observances that aren't too difficult or time-consuming—and never to the point that they will intrude upon their normally comfortable lifestyle.

LOVING, FAITHFUL, PROTECTIVE

Giraffes often have a way of finding and winning wealthy spouses who can make their lives easier and more pleasant. When they enter a relationship, Giraffes are often shy, but they can and often do make their needs and desires known, fully expecting their wishes to be fulfilled. Giraffes seek serenity and harmony, trying hard to maintain domestic tranquility and making life as pleasant as possible for everyone in the household. Their loving nature makes them nurturing and faithful mates, and they generally make excellent parents. In fact, the only time Giraffes become overtly confrontational is when they or a member of their family is being seriously threatened. In such a case, you'll see normally mild-mannered Giraffes become ferocious fighters in defense of themselves or the people they love.

LOVE BEING IN LOVE

Giraffes are romantic, generous, and caring, but they can also make moody lovers, since they have a tendency to worry about how to maintain the comfort, peace, and stability they long for in their lives. To win a Giraffe's heart, sentimentality and romantic gestures will work best. Soft candlelight, beautiful music, and thoughtful, romantic gifts are always appreciated. Giraffes often look at the world through rose-colored glasses and love to be in love—especially if they're secure in their partner's faithfulness and sincerity. The best thing you can do as a lover is to let your Giraffe know how much you love and appreciate them—and that they can always count on their love and affection being reciprocated. When Giraffes feel happy and secure, everyone around them will experience a harmonious existence, full of peace and joy.

CAN BE REMOTE, WITHDRAWN

Giraffes enjoy giving generous gifts when they feel good about themselves and their world, but when they're not feeling loved or appreciated, they can often drift away, both emotionally and physically. Since they don't like conflict, they usually withdraw from difficult situations rather than debate—but never make the mistake of thinking that withdrawal means a Giraffe is giving in. They may not disagree with you on the surface, but if Giraffes don't believe in your cause, they won't follow you, even though you may never know the reason why if you don't ask them directly—and in a non-threatening way.

TEAM PLAYERS WITH STRINGS

Giraffes are renowned for being excellent team players, and as long as they feel as if they're a valued and respected member of your team, you can count on them to be there when you need them. As long as you never disregard their emotional need for respect and appreciation, your Giraffe will take excellent care of you.

SENSITIVE

Giraffes are some of the most creative people on the planet, as well as being some of the most elegant, charming, and artistic. They have an innate love of nature that causes them to seek out not only beauty within themselves and their homes, but in the natural world, as well. They simply need to surround themselves with things they find beautiful, which includes a loving relationship with someone who can understand and appreciate them for the wonderful, talented, sensitive people they really are. Luckily, Giraffes are such disarming people that they are generally surrounded by people who are perfectly willing to do just that.

When it comes to compatibility, Giraffes are probably the most versatile and compatible animals. Under the right conditions and with the right person, a Giraffe can get along with almost any other animal type. However, their most compatible animals are Tree Frogs, Warthogs, and Zebras. On the other hand, Gorillas or Hippos often find Giraffes too passive for their tastes, and the logical Water Buffalo will soon lose patience with the sometimes flighty and irresponsible Giraffe. Since Giraffes are often pessimists at heart (which goes a long way to explain their constant need for love, respect, and appreciation) Giraffes don't generally mix well with Elephants—in either love relationships or business situations.

Hippo

Animal Number Five

AMIABLE, WITTY, INTELLIGENT

Although Hippos have often received a bad rap over the centuries for being moody and unpredictable, the truth is that Hippo people are some of the most amiable and witty individuals you'll ever meet—if you don't needlessly provoke them. Their natural charm and affability attracts people to them, which means Hippos usually enjoy a considerable amount of popularity. Hippos may not talk a great deal, but they're perfectly comfortable in the spotlight and aren't easily ignored. In fact, Hippos generally seek out the limelight—or more accurately, the limelight seeks them—and they seem to thrive on public recognition. Hippos aren't particularly loud or outspoken, but their natural charm and charisma, coupled with an inordinate amount of intelligence and a distinctly philosophical bent, just seems to thrust them into the public eye without their having to work hard to gain that attention.

ATTRACTIVE, SEDUCTIVE

If anything, Hippos can sometimes suffer from being too attractive. People find themselves naturally drawn to Hippos and fall hopelessly in love with them, sometimes in spite of themselves. For that reason, Hippos sometimes can find themselves somewhat oversexed simply because of the availability of willing partners. In matters of the heart, Hippos can be romantic and charming. Perhaps that's why they've gained such a reputation for being sexy and seductive.

PRONE TO JEALOUSY

Their sense of humor is an added asset in attracting members of the opposite sex, but once Hippos choose their partners, they can be somewhat jealous and possessive—even with partners they no longer love. Since they're used to being loved and sought after, the worst blow

Hippos can suffer is rejection. Though they're attractive and vivacious, their egos are fragile. Hippos need to be accepted if they're going to feel good about themselves and the world around them.

LOGICAL, INTUITIVE, PATIENT

When it comes to finally selecting a life partner, Hippos use their characteristic logic and intuition to do their best to pick the perfect mate. Only the best will do, which means that Hippos often wait longer to take the plunge than other animals. They're elegant people themselves, so they generally choose elegant mates. Once they've made their decision, they will work tirelessly to win that person's heart. However, once they've won that person's affection, their possessiveness can make life difficult for both mates. Hippos are very passionate, but demanding, lovers.

LIFELONG STRUGGLE WITH SEX-APPEAL

Since they're so attractive to the opposite sex, Hippos are often tempted to pursue extramarital affairs. Unless they can learn to continually direct their affection toward their mate, they'll face a lifetime of struggle, because people will just naturally continue coming on to them. If Hippos can get a handle on that situation, they can eventually become excellent mates and great parents.

PERSEVERANT, WELL-DEVELOPED SIXTH SENSE

Hippos make decisions quickly and then stick to their guns and will follow through on projects until they're completed. When deliberating, Hippos often rely more heavily on their first impressions, instincts, and feelings rather than on cold, hard facts or the advice of other people. When it comes to decision making, Hippos turn to their well-developed sixth sense—something that can be hard for other people to understand, which can make them seem somewhat mysterious and otherworldly to people who don't know them well. Hippos may be quite interested in religion, mysticism, or the occult.

EASY MONEY, CONTROLLING LENDERS

When it comes to money, Hippos generally don't worry. Money just seems to be there when it's needed. Hippos can sometimes be stingy with their money, however, if you appeal to their logic as well as their sympathetic nature, they often loosen up and can be quite generous—especially with friends and family. Hippos aren't true misers—they're just cautious when it comes to their finances. However, they can show an odd possessiveness toward people they've helped that can be a bit stifling, so you may want to think twice before asking for a loan from a Hippo.

SUCCESSFUL, LUCKY, CEREBRAL

In business, Hippos are often successful and lucky, since their fortunes depend upon a combination of using their logic to make careful judgments, and on their intuition to recognize opportunities to make significant amounts of money quickly. Hippos don't particularly like to work hard, but their laser-quick minds help them make money without having to overtax themselves. They're more likely to pursue professions that allow them to use their minds than those that require a great deal of physical effort. They can make excellent politicians because their calculating minds allow them to debate anything logically and persuasively. They can also make fine lawyers.

PRONE TO HYPERBOLE, CARRY GRUDGES

Hippos have a tendency to exaggerate— sometimes to a significant degree. Though they don't lie often, they can tell whoppers on occasion if they think they can get away with it, which can get them into trouble. They can also be fickle, and they will sometimes be tempted to double-cross other people in an effort to save themselves. If you offend or break your promise with Hippos, you may find that they'll carry a grudge against you for a long time. Although they may stretch the truth at times, they expect you to be straightforward and honest. When Hippos are upset with someone, they're more likely to give them the silent treatment than to lash out with angry words.

HARD WORKING, SELF DISCIPLINED

When Hippos believe in a project, they'll work very hard to finish it. They have a natural ability to remain calm, even in the midst of a crisis, which inspires others to remain calm, as well—long enough to diffuse the situation. They have a tremendous amount of self-discipline that, when coupled with their physical attractiveness and winning personalities, generally allows them to reach great heights in their chosen fields.

LOVE ART, FINE THINGS

Hippos are often art lovers and have a strong appreciation for the finer things in life. You're much more likely to find an original piece of artwork in their homes than an imitation. Their love of the good life is legendary and they enjoy

---

collecting things that interest them. They like elegant homes and surround themselves with beautiful things, including other beautiful people, who also love being around them simply because of the charm and elegance that Hippos naturally possess.

As for compatibility among members of the opposite sex, Hippos will generally do best to seek out Tree Frogs, Giraffes, and Elephants. However, you'll find yourself annoyed for no clearly discernable reason when you have to spend much time in the company of Geckos or Parrots. In business, you may find a strong partner in a Zebra.

Lion

Animal Number Six

BORN LEADERS

Lions are born leaders and are the kinds of people who are most likely to rally others to take up their cause by shouting, "The time is right to take action! Now everyone follow me!"

COURAGEOUS, FEARLESS

Other people instinctively look up to Lions because of their quiet courage—and their greatest admirers are often people who are on the other side of a particular issue at any given time. Lions are fearless warriors who will strongly stand up and fight for their ideals until the bitter end. They have magnetic personalities that can be difficult for people to resist, and their natural air of quiet confidence causes people to follow them instinctively.

UNPREDICTABLE, FILLED WITH CONTRAST

Although they're often seen as quite attractive on the outside, Lions are often looked upon by those who know them as people of distinct, sometimes dramatic contrasts. They can be unpredictable, and although they're capable of being extremely generous to those they love, they can also be selfish in petty ways at times. There will be times when they're troubled on the inside, but even during those times they'll display a disarming sense of calm strength on the outside. Their behavior may be hard to predict, but deep down, Lions have soft, warm hearts. They are capable of showing unbelievable courage, yet they have soft spots inside of them that can show up at the most unusual moments.

OVERLY CONFIDENT

If they have one fault, it's that Lions can sometimes be too confident for their own good, but they can't seem to help it. They love adventure and love to be in charge. Knowing that, if you find yourself living with a Lion, it's best not to challenge them directly. You may find yourself in for a fierce fight unless you approach your Lion with caution and intelligence.

HARDWORKING

Lions may often seem to be in a hurry, but that's only because Lions are doers by nature. They want to get things done and done right, which often means they have to do those things themselves—and what better time to do something than the present? Lions are hardworking and when you give Lions tasks to perform, no matter how difficult or complicated, they'll attack them with a combination of efficiency and tireless enthusiasm.

NATURALLY ATTRACT $$$

When it comes to their finances, Lions often make a considerable amount of money, but it's not because making money is the focus of their lives. In fact, Lions aren't even particularly interested in making money—money just seems to come to them as a natural by-product of their leadership skills, sharp minds, and willingness to work hard. Lions don't seem to worry about money. Somehow money always shows up in their lives at exactly the time when it's needed, and in more than sufficient quantity.

PASSIONATE LOVERS,
CAN BE POSSESSIVE

Because of their quiet confidence, physical attractiveness, and understated sensuality, Lions often exude an allure to the opposite sex that can be hard to resist. However, although Lions may seem fierce and intimidating on the outside, they're generally sensitive and emotional at heart. They're capable of loving deeply and passionately, but can sometimes be too intense and overly possessive. Lions expect their lovers to stand by their side in solidarity against the bad things in the world, and as lovers, the biggest challenge for Lions is to grasp the concept of moderation in all things—including love. Lions can have strong libidos and are often flirtatious and prone to wild flings in their early years—although they do tend to settle down as they mature. When involved in a happy and fulfilling relationship, Lions are generally warm, generous, caring lovers—even though they will always retain the ability to surprise their mates.

BLIND TO DANGER

Lions naturally attract followers and make good leaders, but their passion can sometimes get them into trouble, since they have a tendency to rub authority figures the wrong way. Since they believe in themselves so strongly, Lions are sometimes blind to the true dangers of a situation and rush into places where less impetuous people would fear to tread. However, when Lions are fighting for an altruistic cause, they can be eloquently outspoken because their strong humanitarian beliefs won't allow them to stand idly by while a wrong is being committed.

HONEST, OPEN

Lions prefer an unfettered lifestyle and tend to choose careers that will allow them to enrich their lives and widen their perspective through a variety of meaningful experiences. In fact, Lions value experience above the accumulation of material wealth. Their approach toward life revolves around honesty and openness, and everyone they meet can immediately sense their kindness and quiet generosity. However, when backed into a corner, Lions are legendary for their incredible ability to overcome any obstacle with a combination of fierceness and bravery. Even so, when not faced with a crisis situation, Lions are generally known for possessing a well-developed sense of humor.

SOLITARY

Lions may find themselves living solitary lives, but they eventually become aware that it's the inevitable price they have to pay for being true to themselves and their nature—and with that acceptance comes an increased inner strength and energy that can be channeled to perform great things in the world.

LIFE: ADVENTURE AND OPPORTUNITY

When Lions are injured, whether emotionally or physically, they expect all-out sympathy from the people around them. Just as they do when they're in love, Lions put everything they have into experiencing pain when they're faced with it. They want to be comforted and will respond favorably when you sincerely offer it to them. Since they're charismatic people, Lions usually have a number of people who are eager to offer the sympathy they need in times of trouble and pain. However, no matter how difficult the situation, Lions will eventually bounce back with courage and vitality. To a Lion, life is an

THE DATING JUNGLE
101

---

adventure, and having to start over is merely an exciting new opportunity to make a fresh start.

CONFIDENT IN THEIR DECISIONS

Lions are willing to listen to logic and advice, but only as a means by which to arrive at their own decision about a situation. Once they've weighed all the available advice, they'll go out and do exactly as they please, based on the outcome of their deliberations. However, once a decision has been made, Lions will work tirelessly toward bringing about a positive outcome for everyone involved.

Lions will get along best with Geckos and Warthogs. However, there is one animal they should avoid above all—the Water Buffalo. Since Water Buffaloes are much stronger than Lions, they will continue to attack Lions until they're destroyed. Lions are so brave, however, that they will often put up an incredible fight, but if they're going to survive a relationship with Water Buffaloes, Lions will have to leave in order to save themselves from destruction.

Tree Frog
Animal Number Seven

KIND, SWEET, CONSERVATIVE, INSECURE

Since Tree Frogs are generally kind and sweet people, they're usually popular people, as well. They're among the luckiest and most creative types of people. They make great companions and know how to take care of themselves, their friends, and families. They're conservative, as a rule, and basically insecure, even though they have a strong belief in themselves and their own innate ability, which may explain why they're not terribly fond of change.

REFINED, EASY TO LIKE

Tree Frogs are renowned for their good taste and artistic sense, and they love to look nice in their personal appearance. They also love to decorate their homes beautifully. As a result of their refinement and calm sense of self-assurance, Tree Frogs are one of the happiest animals, too. They're refined and virtuous, and they make such good company that it's almost impossible to ignore them. Their warm personalities make them easy to like, and even after Tree Frogs have had a disagreement with someone, that person will quickly forgive and forget, because Tree Frogs are so disarming that the original cause of the disagreement is soon a distant memory.

CALM, SERENE, AVOID CONFLICT

Tree Frogs don't like conflict, so it's hard to provoke an argument with them. They like calm, serene lives with as few problems as possible. When faced with a difficulty, Tree Frogs will weigh all the aspects of the problem before making a decision. That generally makes them successful in their undertakings because they don't just rush into a situation without carefully weighing the pros and cons.

EXCELLENT PARENT, SENSUAL

In romance, Tree Frogs can make great partners. They're romantics at heart, sweet and faithful, though they can be picky when it comes to choosing a mate. They often look for someone who is attractive, sensual, yet can provide a pleasant life filled with creature comforts. However, once they make their choice, they can make wonderful parents and spouses, fully devoting their lives to making a happy home. Their sensual nature often leads to rather large families, as well. Tree Frogs can be sentimental and sometimes wear their hearts on their sleeve, but they're compassionate and make good listeners if you have something you need to talk about. Being emotional and sensitive, Tree Frogs can be moved to tears easily at times.

AVOID CONFLICT

In business, Tree Frogs do best when they learn to control their sentimental, laid-back nature and get a bit more aggressive. Their quick minds allow them to recognize opportunities, but they're prone to abandon projects before they're completed. Tree Frogs tend to bypass obstacles rather than tackling them head-on, and avoiding conflict allows them to remain calm and not have to show an undue amount of hostility or aggression. Their natural ability to sum up situations quickly makes them excellent negotiators. They look at obstacles and work around them rather than trying to bulldoze their way through.

NAÏVE BUT SHREWD

Since Tree Frogs are so calm and cool, they are sometimes looked upon as being aloof. People may see them as quirky and eccentric, but Tree Frogs are always thinking, trying to see the most efficient, least aggressive way to accomplish their goals. Even though they may appear naïve and vulnerable, Tree Frogs are born with an innate intelligence that generally puts them several steps ahead of their competition. They're shrewd and streetwise, even though you'd never know it by looking at them.

ARTISTIC, LOVE FASHION

Since Tree Frogs have a strong love of the good life, they're often drawn to the arts. They have refined tastes and are often talented artists in their own right. They're highly creative themselves, so they're naturally drawn to other artistic people. They're often collectors of artwork, decorating their homes with paintings, sculpture, and other artistic creations—and they especially like displaying their own work. Tree Frogs also like to look nice, so they have a tendency toward upscale clothing and you can usually pick them out in a crowd by the way they dress. Either they'll be in the latest fashion or they'll make a fashion statement of their own by creating their own unique look.

DISARMING, LIKE WIN-WIN SOLUTIONS

Since they detest drama and conflict, Tree Frogs want nothing to do with war or anything to do with exceptional adversity. They don't make especially good politicians or lawyers because they don't like to debate face-to-face. When it comes to negotiating, however, they're very effective because their disarming affability makes other people eager to work with them. Tree Frogs seek win-win situations, not all-out victories at all costs. When you enter a negotiation with Tree Frogs, they'll show an extraordinary concern for making compromises that will benefit both sides, and before you know it, you've signed the paperwork, almost as if you've been mesmerized—which, in fact, you have, although Tree Frogs would never admit that was the case.

LOVE PEACE, NOT WAR

If Tree Frogs have a motto in life, it would be, "To each, his own." They believe in live and let live, and if you try to push them or bully them, you'll often find that your Tree Frogs have disappeared rather than allowing you to treat them that way. That's one reason Tree Frogs don't have very many enemies. They simply refuse to get caught up in another person's conflict. Life is too short for conflict, as far as Tree Frogs are concerned. When a situation gets too complicated or threatening, Tree Frogs can get unpredictable, so you may not be able to count on them in a crisis. Tree Frogs will listen to your problems and offer you a great deal of sympathy, but it's unrealistic to expect them to take a bullet for you. It's nothing personal—it's just not in their nature. They're not fighters, even though they're generally wonderful negotiators and peacekeepers.

CREATIVE, NEED UNDERSTANDING

Tree Frogs are usually good hosts and can be excellent entertainers, as well. In fact, their sympathetic creative side often allows them to become great actors, authors, or songwriters. They believe in themselves implicitly and that belief brings them a strong sense of inner peace. As long as they find careers that allow them to capitalize on that strength, they'll do well in life. The same goes for mates—if they find someone who understands their gentle nature and creative peacefulness, they'll lead happy, contented lives.

When it comes to compatibility with other animals, Tree Frogs do best with Elephants and Warthogs. Giraffes might also make good possibilities, because they have an innate understanding of a Tree Frog's sensitivity and artistic bent that allows Tree Frogs the freedom to become all they can be—with the least amount of conflict and judgment.

However, Tree Frogs should generally avoid Zebras, Lions, and Geckos.

Warthog

Animal Number Eight

LIVE TO PLEASE

When you first meet Warthogs, they can sometimes seem too good to be true. You can actually feel their sincerity and purity from the way they talk and act. They're tolerant, sincere, honest, and honorable. They show a great deal of care to people around them, and they can always be trusted to do their very best not to let you down. They live their lives to please others and are living examples that chivalry is definitely not dead. Everyone seems to admire Warthogs, and for good reason. They represent the best of our giving nature.

BELIEVE IN THE GOODNESS OF OTHERS

Warthogs can get fooled, but they don't let it faze them. After all, they figure, they were put on this earth to serve humanity and they give without thinking about it—sometimes to the point of being taken advantage of. Even as they mature, Warthogs somehow manage to maintain a strong belief in the basic goodness of human beings and derive their greatest joy from sacrificing their own comforts for the sake of others.

CANNOT ACCEPT FAVORS

Warthogs make great friends, unless you do something that makes them disapprove of you. Don't try to force your ideas on your Warthog friends, and don't work too hard to do things for them because although they love to give, they often have a hard time receiving help or favors graciously. It just makes them uncomfortable.

GREAT CONVERSTAIONALISTS, LOVE FINE DINING

Warthogs are generally soft-spoken, but once you get them talking, they can hold up their end of the conversation without difficulty. They are intellectual people and possess a healthy thirst for knowledge. Warthogs can sometimes come across as a bit snobbish, but that's only because they place a high value on good manners, breeding, and taste. Warthogs have an innate sense of style and have a special place in their hearts for fine dining. Even when Warthogs eat too much, they do it with style and grace.

SWEET, ROMANTIC BUT POSSESSIVE AND JEALOUS

When it comes to romance, Warthogs can be very sensitive and sweet, but they're often naïve and can be overpossessive and jealous. They are romantics at heart and love to be involved in romantic relationships. Although they can be quite genteel and stylish on the outside, Warthogs can show a surprisingly risqué side when it comes to lovemaking.

Younger Warthogs can tend to be somewhat promiscuous, simply because they are passionate by nature. Unfortunately, love can cloud their judgment and love-struck Warthogs can sometimes get hurt deeply by people who take advantage of their trusting nature. Warthogs have a tendency to want to please, which can sometimes prove devastating in affairs of the heart.

AVOID ATTENTION

Warthogs are honest to a fault—in fact, they feel guilty if they make the slightest error and are actually more tolerant and forgiving of others when they make mistakes than they are of themselves. Warthogs don't like being the center of attention—it makes them uncomfortable. However, although they don't seek the limelight, they can be tireless in their efforts to help others become the best they can be.

HONEST, UPFRONT, OPEN

Chivalrous, obliging, and scrupulous, Warthogs also accept their own faults graciously and tolerate those of others with patience and understanding. They are so honest and forthright that they are sometimes taken aback when they don't receive such treatment in return. They are naïve enough to sometimes miss hypocrisy in other people. They always deal from the top of the deck, and since they're so honest, they rarely have to compromise to get what they want. Their cards are on the table, and you don't have to wonder if they're holding anything back in a negotiation.

PERFECTIONISTS

Warthogs can sometimes be a bit extravagant because they love the good life and take delight from spoiling themselves and those they love. They love experiences involving all the senses. That doesn't mean they aren't willing to work hard. On the contrary, they will work tirelessly until they get a job done right—and their standards of perfection are higher than average. Halfway won't do for a Warthog.

INTELLIGENT BUT BAWDY

Since Warthogs are thirsty for knowledge, they often are avid readers. However, they are sometimes indiscriminate in what they read—they'll read whatever happens to be at hand at any given moment. That can sometimes result in acquiring a great deal of rather superficial knowledge. Although Warthogs are intelligent and cultured, they can display a surprising bawdy streak at times. They can also go through periods in which they seem to lose interest in life and can gain weight and become somewhat lazy. Eventually, however, they find a cause to work on and a way to serve that reignites their lust for life.

FAITHFUL FRIEND

Warthogs are generally practical, down-to-earth people. They're sometimes mistaken for being rather cold and reserved because they are able to keep their emotions in check and stay cool in stressful situations. Around people they're comfortable with, they're cheerful and love to entertain socially. They make friends easily because their innocent demeanor is so disarming. Once Warthogs accept someone as a friend, they'll do anything they can to help that person.

WEIGH ALL OPTIONS

Warthogs will do their duty and do it with everything they have inside them—which is considerable. They possess an incredible amount of inner strength that is virtually unstoppable. Once a Warthog has reached a decision, it will be carried out—without question.

However, before that decision is reached, Warthogs will examine every aspect of the situation, which can sometimes look like indecision—but that's not the case. Warthogs will weigh the pros and cons carefully and then move forward with gusto once a decision has been reached.

GOOD PROVIDERS

Warthogs do well when they are their own boss. Given their love of the finer things, they can make excellent art or antique dealers. When it comes to creature comforts, Warthogs will always provide well for themselves and their families.

Somehow money just seems to come to them without having to make any special effort. Since people can sense their sincerity and honesty, they're willing to trust them with their business. The only thing that holds Warthogs back in finances is the size of their goals.

VICIOUS WHEN CORNERED, FIRM FRIEND

Although Warthogs are generally tolerant and docile, they can be vicious fighters when backed into a corner. This is especially true once they discover that they've been duped or abused. When that happens, they will lash out with a fury that can be surprising. Warthogs value friendship above all things. They are loyal and loving, and their capacity for caring for those they love is almost impossible to measure. If they can find the right mate, they will enjoy happy lives, helping their lover to become everything they can be.

Warthogs are most compatible with Tree Frogs, Geckos, Giraffes, and Gorillas. They have more choices than most other animals simply because of their loving and giving nature.

All in all, Warthogs make great friends, lovers, and companions, but they need to avoid being coupled with Hippos, who are strong and cunning enough to make their lives miserable.

Warthogs can also find themselves being used by Giraffes, and Chimpanzees aren't honest enough for Warthogs, who abhor hypocrisy and even the whitest of lies.

Zebra

Animal Number Nine

PARTY ON

Zebras are energetic and active people. They love crowds, which may explain why they love going to the theatre, concerts, sporting events—and parties.

QUICK AND CUNNING

They have quick minds and will often be way ahead of you by the time you even finish a sentence. However, Zebras have more cunning and common sense than intelligence, which means they sometimes can appear to be slow—and they often use that to their advantage in bargaining situations.

INDEPENDENT, HOT-HEADED

Zebra people are independent and high-spirited, which means they often leave home earlier than other people. They like the freedom to move around and even to live fast at times, and they often love to travel. They can be hot-headed and impatient at times, which can sometimes cost them dearly.

LONERS WITH AMBITION

Zebras are sometimes not team players. They have a great deal of ambition and energy, but they often are loners and hate being pressured to do something that is for the good of the team— especially if you use guilt as a way of trying to persuade them. They also have a tendency to get caught up in their own problems to the exclusion of others. Their ego sometimes gets the better of their judgment. Paradoxically, by working diligently to resolve their own problems, Zebras often bring about tremendous benefits to the overall group.

TIRELESS WORKER

Zebras can be tireless workers, especially when it comes to things they really believe in, and they're generally adept at handling their finances. On the other hand, Zebras are notorious for losing interest in a project on a moment's notice.

ILLOGICAL IN LOVE

When it comes to romance, Zebras have a great deal of innate sex appeal and they know how to dress in order to take fullest advantage of their physical attributes. When Zebras fall in love, however, they will give everything up for the object of their affection. In a strange way, Zebras become weaker when they're in love. Zebras can often have a touch of arrogance, but they're surprisingly modest when it comes to their love relationships. They want to be loved and crave intimacy, but they hate feeling cornered or pressured. When they fall in love, Zebras often seem to lose their sense of perspective and can become downright illogical at times. Although Zebras can be unpredictable at any time of their lives, falling in love makes them even less predictable.

INDEPENDENT, BUT NEED SECURITY

If you love a Zebra, make sure to keep the mood light and don't apply too much pressure. Zebras treasure their independence and coupled with a low threshold for boredom, they can be difficult to hold on to. So don't make too many demands on their freedom if you want to keep your Zebra around. They're eccentric free thinkers and love adventure. They love heartily, but they often end up married several times before they find the one person who can give them what they really need—a combination of freedom and security. If you can hold on to them long enough, Zebras generally mellow with age and become much more stable later in life.

CAPABLE OF PROVING THEMSELVES

Zebras are proud and somewhat egotistic, and they have a well-developed stubborn streak—to the point of sometimes being selfish. However, their basic nature is sweet, tolerant, and humble, even though they can be a bit conceited about their appearance. Zebras may be independent, but they often harbor a secret desire to belong—and that dichotomy can sometimes lead to a tortured soul. Zebras rely on their wits and hard labor to get what they want, and they feel good when they're able to prove to themselves—and to the people they love—that they can do it alone if they have to. Since they are tireless in their pursuit of their goals, Zebras often end up financially secure.

EASY-GOING, BUT PAINFULLY HONEST

Zebras generally have a well-developed sense of humor and are very congenial. Their amiable, easy-going personalities help them attract lots of friends, partly because they're able to instantly put strangers at ease. Ironically, their major personality flaw turns out to be their intense honesty. Zebras will speak their minds and be totally frank when asked their opinion, which can sometimes be mistaken for tactlessness by other people.

EASILY BORED

Freedom is essential to Zebras. They love exercise, both mental and physical—they must have room to run and hate being tied down. Their threshold for boredom is low, so they sometimes move within a sizable number of friends in order to remain stimulated. They'll also move from hobby to hobby or sometimes job to job in order to maintain their interest in life. Since they get bored easily, Zebras can be unpredictable because the moment they get bored, they instinctively seek out something else to occupy their minds.

EXTROVERTS EXTRAORDINAIRE

When it comes to careers, Zebras can do most anything that involves people, but they don't like working alone or having to spend hours puzzling out a problem. They're extroverts and work best in social situations, surrounded by people.

HIGH-SPIRITED, HOT-TEMPERED

Zebras are comfortable on center stage and can make excellent entertainers. They're high-spirited and vivacious, and their enthusiasm for life makes them popular. However, their moods can change quickly. At times, they can display unsavory flashes of temper. People who have felt the sting of a Zebra's rage will be wary of that person from that moment on, wondering if it will ever happen again—especially since the outbursts are often somewhat childish. If Zebras truly want to succeed in life, they need to learn to master their tempers.

PERSUASIVE, MOODY, UNIQUE

Zebras often make good politicians, because they get plenty of opportunities to plainly speak their minds. Their winning personality also gives them an above average ability to persuade people—especially large groups of people. They're also great debaters because of their ability to quickly size up situations. Zebras often make business decisions by following their hunches, and their quick wits and intuition are legendary. However, just as they do in love relationships, Zebras can change moods quickly and lose interest—which can lead to unfinished projects or even complete career changes at the drop of a hat. Zebras will throw themselves into whatever they do next with all their inherent enthusiasm, especially jobs in which they're given a free hand to pursue their own unique fashion.

When it comes to compatibility, Zebras will generally do best with Giraffes, Lions, and Elephants. Giraffes are especially well suited to Zebras because they think alike in many ways. Lions and Elephants are also good possibilities because they will be tolerant of a Zebra's occasional bouts of instability. However, Zebras are generally not compatible with Geckos—such a union can often be incendiary because of their similarly passionate nature, which will eventually cause both of them to go down in flames.

Parrot

Animal Number Ten

ECCENTRIC, CONTRADICTORY, UNIQUE

Parrots are some of the most eccentric people you'll ever meet. They are a bundle of contradictions and they will generally have a style all their own. They're not only full of dreams and romantic ideas, but they're also organized and practical at the same time. They're proud of their appearance, but they're basically conservative deep inside. They love challenges, but when pushed beyond their ability to cope, they'll suddenly retreat.

WELL-DEVELOPED SIXTH SENSE

Parrots are known for their powers of observation, and most of the time their decisions about the things they see and hear are right on the money. In fact, Parrots have an uncanny sixth sense that helps them see the world more clearly than other people.

DESIRE FLATTERY AND NOTICE

Parrots are also transparent in their character—in other words, what you see is what you get—at least in terms of the things they say. They're not particularly complicated people, but they are very upfront and honest. You can nearly always believe everything they tell you. On the outside, however, Parrots can be a bit flashy and like to be noticed and flattered. Paradoxically, Parrots may dress colorfully, but they're actually fairly conservative at the core of their being. They're social people and use their outward flashiness to attract attention.

HARD TO DECEIVE

With their keen observation skills and innate instincts for spotting phonies, Parrots are hard to deceive. They're easily able to solve problems—in fact, they love doing that—so they're often drawn to careers that involve problem solving, such as technicians, detectives, lawyers, doctors, or nurses. However, they make poor negotiators because they clearly and openly speak their minds and strongly believe in the positions they're taking.

ALWAYS BUSY

You'll rarely see Parrots sitting in the living room vegetating like a couch potato. If they're watching TV, they're usually doing something else at the same time, such as a craft project, talking on the phone, or something else they can easily use to multitask.

BARGAIN HUNTERS

Just because they like to look nice doesn't mean that Parrots are careless with their finances. They also love to compare prices and to find bargains. Even if they only save a little on something, it makes them feel better. In fact, managing their finances is one of their greatest strengths. When it comes to money, Parrots are prudent and cautious.

DREAMERS

Parrots also have a tendency to be dreamers, which can be hard on their love life because reality hardly ever matches the sweetness and light of a dream. That can be a very difficult standard to live up to if you fall in love with a Parrot.

SOMEWHAT VAIN

Parrots enjoy the company of the opposite sex and appreciate being told how nice they look, since that's one of their greatest pleasures—at heart, Parrots are somewhat vain about their appearance. Male Parrots generally prefer the company of women and don't go in much for nights out with the boys. Female Parrots, on the other hand, prefer the company of women, but they also love men and often choose professions that put them in touch with men on a regular basis.

LACK OF COMMITMENT

Parrots make judgments quickly, which means they're prone to falling in love at first sight. Their love life can be exciting, though they have a tendency to want to dominate their partner, even if it's mostly for show. Parrots can be quite passionate and often possess an active sex drive, but they can sometimes lack a firm commitment when it comes to entering serious relationships. This lack of commitment can strain a relationship when coupled with the fact that Parrots also feel the need to be continually reminded that they're attractive to the opposite sex. However, the good news is that when a Parrot does fully commit, you won't have to worry because honesty is very important to a Parrot, including fidelity. They may like to be flattered, but Parrots are generally loyal and faithful once they've committed themselves to someone.

DEPENDABLE

Parrots make devoted friends, as well. They always keep their promises and when they give you their word, you can take it to the bank. They're resourceful, courageous, hardworking, and talented, which also makes them self-assured people. They impress people with their magnetic personalities and they're generally vivacious and popular.

VERY ORGANIZED

Parrots can sometimes get themselves into trouble because of their inherent vanity and strong egos, which combine to push Parrots toward being in the limelight. You'll often see them as the life of the party, although they can sometimes be too outspoken and blunt in their comments. They like to keep things in perspective and orderly, and they'll sometimes drive friends, family, and coworkers crazy by continually organizing things. Although they have quick minds, Parrots will often consider all sides of a situation before reaching a conclusion. During a conflict, they'll push their cause to the best of their abilities, but if the going gets too difficult, they'll finally back down. That doesn't mean they'll agree with the outcome, but they'll go along, all the while thinking about ways to restructure the situation later on.

When it comes to compatibility, Parrots will generally get along best with Hippos and Water Buffaloes because they're all able to understand how Parrots think, deep down inside. They know that Parrots may be colorful and somewhat over the top on the outside, but are actually relatively reserved beneath that flashy exterior. Chimpanzees and Warthogs also get along relatively well with Parrots, but it's better if they just remain friends or business associates rather than trying to put together a love relationship.

On the other side of the coin, Tree Frogs have a distrust of Parrots and have an inherent distaste for the flashiness and cockiness that Parrots often display. It's best for those two types of people to avoid each other if possible. The most difficult relationship for Parrots is to try to love another Parrot. They will drive each other crazy because they're likely to hurt each other with their constant candor and will become jealous with all the attention each of them gets from the opposite sex. It's been said that everyone in a household will suffer from the union of two Parrots, so when a Parrot tries to love another Parrot, it can be a recipe for disaster.

Gecko

Animal Number Eleven

A STUDY IN CONTRASTS

Geckos are people of contrasts. They are charming but sometimes aggressive; they can be talkative or quiet; they like to attend parties but also enjoy their alone time. Geckos often have more acquaintances than close friends, however, once Geckos include you as a friend, they'll treat you like family. Geckos are often self-oriented and tend to keep their problems to themselves. They may be talkative at times, but it's rare for them to confide their innermost secrets to anyone.

EFFICIENT, PERFECTIONISTS, BUSY

Always on the go, Geckos often accomplish more in a day than many people can do in a week. They're blessed with good instincts and are confident in their own abilities. They're also perfectionists and sometimes stubborn, which can occasionally rub people the wrong way when Geckos insist that a task be done in a very particular way. Geckos prefer to live by their own rules and standards. Geckos like to stay active, both physically and mentally, so they tend to live busy lives. They love to travel, which gives them the stimulation of new experiences and challenges.

PROBLEM SOLVERS, GENEROUS TO A FAULT

Geckos are excellent problem solvers, finding solutions to even the most difficult problems by being organized and efficient. However, when it comes to handling their own finances, none of their positive traits seem to help. They spend their money as fast as it comes in, which means Geckos have to be careful when loaning money, simply because they never quite seem to have enough of it. On the other hand, true to their contrasting nature, Geckos can be very generous with their loved ones. They can also be prone to gambling on get-rich-quick schemes or risky ventures, which can cost them dearly at times.

THRIFTY BARGAIN HUNTER

Since money is often tight, Geckos generally become shrewd shoppers, and one of the things they like best in the whole world is finding a bargain. Even so, they have a sentimental streak that sometimes causes them to buy things they don't need, such as souvenirs from their travels— which they often tuck away and forget when they get home.

LOVING BUT NOT ROMANTIC

When it comes to love relationships, Geckos aren't romantics, but they can be quite sensual and loving. You might not notice a Gecko in a gathering at first, because they don't seek out the limelight, but it's generally well worth your while to take the time to get to know them.

PASSIONATE BUT PUBLICLY ALOOF

Geckos may put up a cool façade, but they can be quite passionate on the inside, and if they love you, you will sometimes be surprised at just how passionate they can be in private. However, they're often perceived to be rather aloof because

---

they don't usually show their deep-seated sensuality and passion in their public persona.

FAMILY ORIENTED

Geckos generally are very family-oriented and are loyal, devoted partners, as well as devoted parents. Their home life means a great deal to them and they will work hard to make life as comfortable for their families as possible—sometimes to the point of wearing down their health in the process. Relatives and good friends are always welcome in a Gecko's house, but if you visit, don't be offended if you're suddenly put to work to help accomplish a task that your Gecko has undertaken.

AVID READERS

Since Geckos love to keep their minds just as active as their bodies, it's not surprising that they're often avid readers who love to accumulate knowledge. They're also able to express themselves well, either orally or through the written word.

HONEST TO A FAULT

You'll find Geckos to be honest to a fault, even though they sometimes can exhibit a mean streak they need to keep under control. Although they often give excellent advice to others, they seem to have difficulty making decisions in their own lives. It's all part of being that creature of contrasts known as a Gecko.

TRY TO DO TOO MUCH

One of the biggest traps that Geckos sometimes fall into is trying to do too many things at once. Since they love being busy, they often find their endurance being tested to its limit as their energy gets scattered. When that happens, frustration can begin to set in because nothing seems to be getting accomplished. However, if Geckos can learn to pace themselves, there is very little that they can't accomplish once they put their minds to it.

GREAT SENSE OF HUMOR

Geckos enjoy a good joke as much as anyone and are well-known among their friends and family members for their excellent sense of humor, even though it may take some coaxing to bring it out. Geckos will laugh and joke around with people they know quite well, but they'll often be relatively quiet and reserved when it comes to unstructured situations where they're surrounded by strangers.

SECRETIVE WITH STRANGERS

If you're involved with a Gecko, you can usually tell when something is wrong. Geckos tend to get edgy and nervous, and they can become nags at times if they don't get their way. They may be somewhat secretive to people they don't know well, but they're fairly good about not keeping their friends and family in the dark about their needs and wants—perhaps too good at times.

GOOD AT SALES, LEVEL-HEADED

Their good memories and inquisitive nature makes Geckos excellent candidates for sales jobs and their problem-solving ability makes them good technicians or IT professionals. They're adaptable people and actually embrace change as it occurs, since it keeps their minds active and stimulated. They also have an uncanny ability to keep their wits about them during a crisis, relying on a combination of level-headed thought and keen intuition to bring a difficult situation under control.

When it comes to seeking out compatible partners, Geckos will do best to look for Gorillas or Chimpanzees. Those two types of people will have the easiest time sorting out the contrasts in a Gecko's internal makeup. On the other hand, Geckos will generally have a difficult time of it if they try to team up with Tree Frogs, who are too impatient to put up with the dichotomy of a Gecko's nature. Even if there's fire between them at the beginning, a relationship between a Gecko and a Tree Frog is generally destined for heartache. The very worst match for a Gecko is a Zebra.

Chimpanzee

Animal Number Twelve

FUN-LOVING, FULL OF LIFE

Chimpanzees are generally easy to spot. They're invariably fun-loving people who are nearly always cheerful and full of life. They're clever people, too, and will rarely miss an opportunity to extract the greatest amount of joy from any given situation. Chimpanzees are talented, creative, and generous souls, which means that they're generally well-liked by just about everyone who meets them.

LIFE OF THE PARTY

Since they're vivacious and gregarious people, you'll usually find that Chimpanzees are the life of the party and perfectly at home in the spotlight. In fact, their outgoing nature, natural charm, and captivating sense of humor practically guarantees that they'll be noticed. That's just the way they are.

HIDE TRUE FEELINGS

On the other hand, a Chimpanzee's outward appearance and actions can be deceptive. In reality, Chimpanzees rarely want to let their true emotions show on the outside, so they sometimes hide their true feelings under a cheerful, friendly exterior. As gregarious as they can be, Chimpanzees simply are uncomfortable with allowing anyone else to see their pain.

GREAT LISTENER

If you have a sticky problem, you can do no better than to call a Chimpanzee friend and ask for advice. They're great listeners and since they are avid learners, as well, they'll listen intently to your problem and then offer sound, knowing advice. From the moment they're born, Chimpanzees are curious by nature, which drives them to continually add to their store of knowledge. Learning is as natural to them as breathing.

INDIFFERENT TO PUBLIC OPINION

Chimpanzees can seem self-centered at times, but that's partly because they don't care too much about how other people judge them—they just go about being who they are, unconcerned with public opinion. That maverick streak makes them different from the majority of the rest of the world, so Chimpanzees stand out, which means they often go farther in the world than their peers. Their inborn charm and wit makes them likable, and people enjoy helping them reach their goals.

FALL IN LOVE EASILY, SOMETIMES FICKLE

Chimpanzees make great friends, but they can be flighty, which can make them somewhat risky as potential love partners. They may fall in love easily, but they often tire of their relationships and begin to look for someone new. This trait can lead to heartache on both sides of the love affair, since Chimpanzees have a hard time maintaining their relationships, even with people they truly love, when their interest begins to fade.

UNSUSTAINABLE PASSION

Chimpanzees often begin love affairs with a considerable amount of torrid passion, but it's not sustainable, which means the fire eventually begins to cool—until it either burns out completely or the Chimpanzee gets bored and begins to seek a new object of excitement. One of the things that helps lessen the pain is the Chimpanzee's excellent sense of humor. Making a lover laugh can prolong a relationship, but it's generally not enough to make it last forever.

REQUIRES CONSTANT STIMULATION

If you can manage to keep your Chimpanzee stimulated, both mentally and physically, you'll have an excellent relationship. The dynamics will be complex at times, but if you're willing to stay with them and constantly work at it, Chimpanzees can be the most amusing, charming, and romantic companions in the world.

LOVE THEIR FAVORITE FOOD

Chimpanzees generally have a fondness for food that is sometimes hard to understand. They don't necessarily like fine cuisine, but they know what they like and tend to throw themselves into the enjoyment of that food with happy abandon. Whether it's sour cream and onion potato chips or fresh fruit, Chimpanzees are devoted to their favorite snacks.

HIGHLY SOCIABLE

Chimpanzees are highly sociable people who can easily hold their own in conversations. Since they're generally well-read and knowledgeable, they can also talk intelligently about a wide variety of subjects, as well. This virtually assures them of a well-rounded circle of friends, which suits Chimpanzees well because they can rarely find one person with whom they can discuss all the different things they're interested in.

INQUISITIVE...OK...NOSY

One thing Chimpanzees have to be aware of is that they can sometimes be too clever for their own good. They may come across as opportunistic and nosey, but that's only because they're so inquisitive that they want to know everything about everybody—and Chimpanzees don't care all that much about what people think anyway.

GLIDE THROUGH LIFE WITH WIT AND CHARM

Chimpanzees also have a tendency to be somewhat lazy. Their winning personalities encourage people to help them, often to the point where Chimpanzees don't need to help themselves very much. Once they realize that they can get nearly anything they want through wit and charm, Chimpanzees can sometimes get quite self-centered and egotistical. They're not particularly good at solving problems because other people are generally quick to step in and lend a hand.

SUCCESSFUL IN BUSINESS

In the world of business, Chimpanzees are often highly successful, partly because they are superb at picking things up quickly. That trait, combined with a winning personality, makes them prime candidates for a quick climb up the ladder of success. Chimpanzees are also fond of money, so their rise in the business world allows them to generate increased income, which they can then use to create a better life for themselves and those they love.

When it comes to finding a compatible love relationship, the gregarious and vivacious Chimpanzees are lucky, as they are in most other parts of their lives. They have more choices than most other animal types, due not in small part to their winning personalities and considerable charm. Geckos will find them especially irresistible and will be interesting enough themselves to maintain a Chimpanzee's interest in return—if they continue to stay with them and keep the relationship fresh. Chimpanzees also will generally get along very well with other Chimpanzees. After all, who is better equipped to understand the sometimes complex thought and feeling processes that go on in the deep recesses of a Chimpanzee's soul than another Chimpanzee? On the other hand, it would be in the best interest of Chimpanzees if they went out of their way to avoid falling in love with Hippos and Zebras. Those two animals view the world very differently and will never quite understand the carefree, devil-may-care Chimpanzee lifestyle—no matter how much charm and wit a Chimpanzee may display.

Compatibility Charts

Water Buffalo
Animal Number One

(From Most Compatible to Least Compatible)

Gecko: Stable and steady relationship

Parrot: Fortunate to find each other

Hippo: Definite potential

Chimpanzee: Compatible and stable relationship

Water Buffalo: Will protect each other

Tree Frog: Not best, but it could work

Warthog: Starting to get iffy here

Elephant: Difficult, but not impossible

Giraffe: Probably won't work

Gorilla: Will fight constantly

Zebra: Unfortunately, they will part

Lion: Not recommended at all

Elephant
-Animal Number Two

(From Most Compatible to Least Compatible)

Zebra: A happy relationship

Lion: Nice balance and harmony

Warthog: Could work, since they share their

feelings

Tree Frog: Could work if both stay cool

Gecko: Could work with compromise

Chimpanzee: Approach with caution, Elephant

may suffer

Hippo: Difficult, but not impossible

Parrot: Will take lots of work

Water Buffalo: Difficult, but not impossible

Gorilla: May want to think again

Giraffe: Will fight, but still might work

Elephant: Too similar, will butt heads

Gorilla
-Animal Number Three-

(From Most Compatible to Least Compatible)

Gecko: Best match

Warthog: Also a good match.

Tree Frog: A good pairing

Chimpanzee: Despite differences, could be fine

Lion: Minor difficulties, but definite potential

Giraffe: Could be stable with lots of work

Parrot: Balanced relationship, but not

passionate

Hippo: Possible, but not recommended

Zebra: Could be love at first sight, but won't

last

Elephant: The Elephant will suffer

Water Buffalo: Will fight constantly

Gorilla: Definitely not; constantly in competition

Giraffe
-Animal Number Four-

(From Most Compatible to Least Compatible)

Warthog: One of the best combinations

Tree Frog: A good coupling

Zebra: Could be volatile, but they won't be bored

Gorilla: Stable, sound relationship

Chimpanzee: Will take work

Hippo: Could work with patience

Elephant: Difficult, but not impossible

Gecko: Not recommended

Giraffe: Best to avoid

Water Buffalo: Might want to just be friends

Parrot: They'll be unhappy, no matter how hard they try

Lion: One of the worst relationships

Hippo
-Animal Number Five-

(From Most Compatible to Least Compatible)

Parrot: A true love connection

Water Buffalo: Could be workable

Zebra: Strong initial attraction, but should be careful

Giraffe: Possible, but not the best

Elephant: Could work with effort

Gecko: Better just to be friends

Lion: Won't see eye to eye

Gorilla: Possible, but not recommended

Tree Frog: Best to think again

Chimpanzee: Not recommended unless Chimpanzee tries very hard

Hippo: Too much drama

Warthog: This will be an unhappy union

Lion
-Animal Number Six-

(From Most Compatible to Least Compatible)

Elephant: A balanced and harmonic match

Zebra: Nice match, lots in common

Chimpanzee: Eager lovers, at least at first

Warthog: Will take lots of work

Gorilla: Will take considerable compromise

Hippo: Hard to see what they see in each other

Gecko: Will take strength and endurance

Parrot: An unbalanced pairing

Lion: Too strong for each other; not

recommended

Tree Frog: A difficult relationship

Giraffe: Not a good combination

Water Buffalo: One of the worst possible

relationships

Tree Frog
-Animal Number Seven-

(From Most Compatible to Least Compatible)

Warthog: Good pairing, should be very happy

Gorilla: Could be a strong relationship

Giraffe: With work, has potential

Elephant: Need to stay low-key to make it work

Chimpanzee: Borderline, approach with care

Tree Frog: Only if there's stable income

involved

Water Buffalo: Best just to be friends

Hippo: Not recommended

Parrot: Won't see eye to eye

Zebra: Will have difficulties

Lion: Not a compatible pairing

Gecko: Definitely not recommended

Warthog
-Animal Number Eight-

(From Most Compatible to Least Compatible)

Giraffe: One of the best possible combinations

Gorilla: Very favorable for longevity

Warthog: A loving, giving relationship

Tree Frog: Quite compatible

Gecko: A good combination with some effort

Elephant: Could work with good communication

Chimpanzee: Mutual admiration at first, harder work later

Lion: Quite different, maybe with compromise

Zebra: Not recommended, but not impossible

Water Buffalo: Not a good match, but possible

Parrot: May work if the Warthog is very patient

Hippo: Not recommended, since a Warthog can never please a Hippo

---

Zebra
-Animal Number Nine-

(From Most Compatible to Least Compatible)

Elephant: A happy couple

Lion: Good match, lots in common

Giraffe: They won't bore each other

Hippo: Strongly attracted to each other

Warthog: Worth a try

Zebra: Each will need to control their egos

Gorilla: Steamy start, but won't last

Parrot: Not recommended without lots of

compromise

Tree Frog: Best just to be friends

Water Buffalo: They won't stay together

Chimpanzee: Not advised

Gecko: Definitely not recommended

Parrot
-Animal Number Ten-

(From Most Compatible to Least Compatible)

Hippo: A healthy love relationship

Water Buffalo: A well-matched couple

Warthog: Warthogs are patient with Parrots

Chimpanzee: Better to remain just friends

Gorilla: Better for friendship than love

Gecko: Can be steamy at first, but won't last

Elephant: Will take great effort

Zebra: Not recommended for loving relationship

Lion: Not a well-balanced union

Giraffe: Both will be unhappy, no matter how
hard they try

Tree Frog: Rarely will work out

Parrot: Entire household will suffer

Gecko
-Animal Number Eleven-

(From Most Compatible to Least Compatible)

Gorilla: One of the best matches

Chimpanzee: Can be a long-lasting relationship

Water Buffalo: Definite potential

Gecko: At least they'll understand each other's

dichotomy

Warthog: They'll at least try to understand

each other

Elephant: Could work, with a lot of effort

Lion: Risky, since they're quite different

Hippo: Better just to be friends

Parrot: Could be steamy at first, but won't last

Giraffe: Not recommended

Tree Frog: Not a good match

Zebra: Definitely not recommended

Chimpanzee
-Animal Number Twelve-

(From Most Compatible to Least Compatible)

Gecko: One of the best relationships

Chimpanzee: Amiable lovers who understand
each other

Gorilla: Can work with considerable effort

Lion: Eager lovers at first, but hard to sustain

Warthog: Mutual admiration, not much passion

Water Buffalo: Good friends, not good lovers

Tree Frog: Good for laughs, not love

Elephant: Best to remain just friends

Parrot: Not recommended

Giraffe: May be fiery at first, but won't last

Hippo: Won't understand each other

Zebra: Definitely not recommended

Animal Tests Tally Sheet

(You might wish to make several photocopies of this so you can capture your future scores more easily; and you can have your friends take the tests, too.)

As you answer the questions for each animal test, place a hash mark in the "Individual 'Yes' Responses" column whenever you answer "Yes" to one of the questions. Before proceeding to the next animal test, tally your "Yes" responses in the third column. Have fun!

Animal Tests	Individual "Yes" Responses	Total "Yes" Responses
Animal # 1		
Animal # 2		
Animal # 3		
Animal # 4		
Animal # 5		
Animal # 6		
Animal # 7		
Animal # 8		
Animal # 9		
Animal # 10		
Animal # 11		
Animal # 12		

Based on the highest tally of "Yes" responses, I am most compatible with Animal Number(s)

The End...

...or, rather...

The Beginning!

www.ingramcontent.com/pod-product-compliance
Lightning Source LLC
LaVergne TN
LVHW021455080426
835509LV00018B/2289